GOLDIE TAKES A STAND!

Golda Meir's First Crusade

For my late mother, Lillian Perlman Krasner,
a strong woman in her own right
– B.K.

For Erik for his unfailing love and support
– K.G.-R.

KAR-BEN PUBLISHING
A division of Lerner Publishing Group, Inc.
241 First Avenue North
Minneapolis, MN 55401 USA
1-800-4-KARBEN

Website address: www.karben.com

Main body text set in Belwe Std Medium 15/20
Typeface provided by Adobe Systems.

Library of Congress Cataloging-in-Publication Data

Krasner, Barbara, author.
    Goldie takes a stand : a story of Golda Meir / by Barbara Krasner ; illustrated by Kelsey Garrity-Riley.
       p.   cm.
     ISBN 978–1–4677–1200–2 (lib. bdg. : alk. paper)
     ISBN 978–1–4677–1202–6 (eBook)
    1. Meir, Golda, 1898-1978—Biography—Juvenile literature. 2. Meir, Golda, 1898-1978—Childhood and youth—Juvenile literature. I. Garrity-Riley, Kelsey, illustrator. II. Title.
    DS126.6.M42K57 2014
    956.94053092aB—dc23   2013022210

Manufactured in the United States of America
1 – VI –7/15/14

GOLDIE TAKES A STAND!

Golda Meir's First Crusade

Barbara Krasner

illustrated by Kelsey Garrity-Riley

KAR-BEN
PUBLISHING

"Will the meeting please come to order?" I announced to the girls crowded into our two-room Walnut Street apartment.

It was the first meeting of the American Young Sisters Society, a group of Jewish immigrants from Russia. I, Goldie Mabowehz, naturally appointed myself president.

In the room was my little sister Clara, my best friend Regina, my neighbor Belle and her sister Frieda, my classmate Lillian, and others.

I had called the meeting to discuss textbooks.

"The kids in our school don't have enough money to buy them," I explained. "They need our help."

"Have you seen Hymie's book?" asked Regina. "He says he's the third person in his family to use it. It's missing half its pages."

"Jennie keeps peeking over my shoulder to see my book," Frieda said. "I wish she'd get her own."

"How much money do we have to raise?" asked Belle.

"Three cents a week," I said, "from each of us." As the best math student in the whole fourth grade, naturally it was up to me to figure this out.

Lillian groaned. "Goldie, that's too much. A loaf of bread costs three cents."

"So does a quart of milk," added Sarah.

"If Goldie thinks we can do it, we can," said Regina.

But when the meeting was over, I wondered where Clara and I would get six cents each week.

Then I knew what to do.

Every morning before school, I worked at Mama's grocery store while she went to the farmer's market.

The next day, when Mrs. Plotkin came to the counter with a quart of milk, I told her, "My friends and I are trying to raise money to buy school books for kids who can't afford them. So your milk will be five cents today, please."

"Your mother only charges three cents!" she protested, but she reached into her purse and handed me a nickel. "Goldie, such a doer you are," she said, pinching my cheek.

"Five cents for the bread," I told Mr. Margolis. "Poor kids need an education." He pulled his worn leather wallet out of his pocket. But four cents was all he had, and I couldn't take it.

I counted Mrs. Garfinkel's eggs. There were six. "Ten cents," I told her. "I'm trying to raise money for school books for kids who can't afford them."

TEXTBOOK FUND!

FOSTER'S BISCUITS

"Harumph! Your mother only charges a penny a piece. That's all I'm paying!" she snapped. She grabbed her eggs and stomped out the door.

But despite all my efforts, at the end of the week, Clara and I still hadn't raised our share. As president of the Society, I listed our options: I could help kids with their math, but no one had money to pay for tutoring. I could get a job as a junior sales girl downtown, but Mama needed me before school, and Clara needed me after.

Then I knew what to do. I decided we would have to give up something we loved.

When Mama gave us each a penny for candy, I told Clara we'd have to do without.

"Do without candy?" Clara sniffled.

I nodded. "Think of the good deed you're doing!" But by the next meeting, no one had raised enough money.

"We need to think bigger," I said. "We'll hold a public meeting, a fundraising gala, and collect from everyone at one time."

"We can make invitations," offered Frieda.

"We can put together a list of important people to invite," suggested Lillian.

"Good ideas," I said. "And naturally, I'll give a speech."

"Where will we put so many people?" Sarah asked.

I knew just what to do.

The next day I headed to Packen Hall, the only place large enough to hold our event.

"What do you want?" a man in a fancy business suit asked me.

"I'm here to see the owner. I need to borrow the hall for a public event," I said.

"You're talking to him."

"I'm Goldie Mabowehz and I'm the president of the American Young Sisters Society." I told him about our cause.

In the end, he donated the hall to us, still shaking his head.

We wrote invitations and painted posters on butcher paper.

All that was left was my speech. And for the first time, I didn't know what to do.

"Write it down," Mama said. "Then you won't forget anything."

Night after night I struggled, but the words wouldn't come.
When the time came, I would just have to speak from my heart.

AMERICAN YOUNG S

The night of our event, I peeked out from behind the Packen Hall stage curtain.

Mama and Papa sat in the front row. The Young Sisters and their parents sat behind them. But where were the rest of the people—people with actual money?

Knots formed in my stomach and throat. But I was president, so I took a deep breath, stepped onto the stage, and began.

"Imagine what it feels like to sit in your classroom without a textbook. You can't follow the teacher. You can't do your work. Education is the only way for us to lift ourselves out of poverty."

I paused when I noticed our school principal push through the double doors in back of the hall and take a seat. The superintendent was with him. Then a handful of teachers appeared. And a sprinkling of parents. Then Mrs. Plotkin and Mr. Margolis. Even Mrs. Garfinkel.

People kept coming. Dozens of them.

"The way we see it," I continued, my voice growing stronger, "it's the community's responsibility to help Milwaukee kids who can't afford school books. I ask each of you to look into your hearts and wallets and give what you can."

When I finished, everyone leaped up and started clapping.

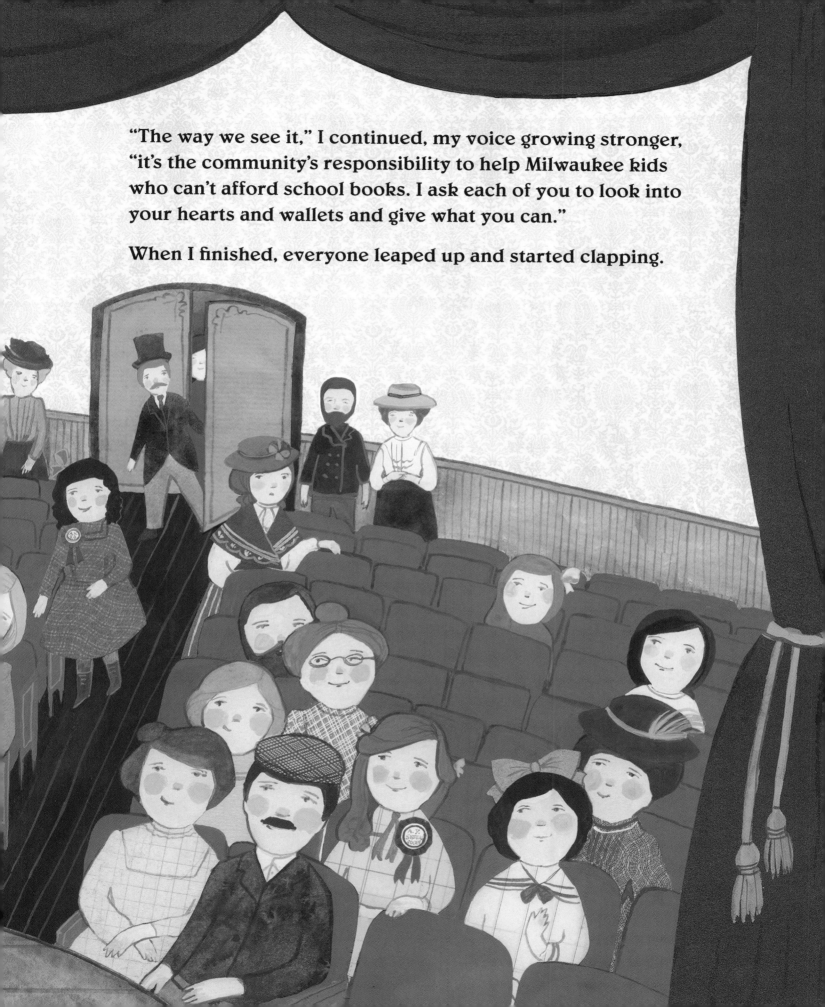

Regina led the Young Sisters through the aisles with their collection baskets. Men pulled out their wallets, women opened their purses, and even Mrs. Garfinkel gave a couple of coins.

"We raised a lot of money," I said as we walked home afterward.

Mama grinned. "I guess that means the American Young Sisters Society is out of business." The truth was, I'd been thinking about a new society — one to raise money to teach English to immigrants. I knew just what to do and naturally-I'd be president!

Golda Meir, age 6

Goldie Meir as Prime Minister of Israel

Goldie Mabowehz (also spelled Mabovitch) was born in Kiev in 1898 and immigrated to Milwaukee with her family in 1906. She trained as a teacher, and with her husband Morris Meyerson went to Palestine in 1921 to help claim it as a Jewish homeland. There, she chose a new last name for herself, Meir, the Hebrew word for "illumination." As Prime Minister of Israel from 1969–1974, she never stopped taking a stand on important issues, and she never wrote down her speeches except when making policy statements to the United Nations or the Israeli Parliament. She died in 1978. The Fourth Street School in Milwaukee was renamed Golda Meir School in her honor.

Although the dialogue in this book is imagined, the events are true. *The Milwaukee Journal* wrote about the American Young Sisters Society's efforts to raise funds for school books for poor children.

PLACES TO VISIT TO LEARN MORE ABOUT GOLDA MEIR

Jewish Museum Milwaukee
1360 N. Prospect Ave.
Milwaukee, WI 53202
www.jewishmuseummilwaukee.org

National Museum of American Jewish History
101 South Independence Mall East
Philadelphia, PA 19106-2517
www.nmajh.org

Golda Meir House/Golda Meir Center for Political Leadership
Metropolitan State College of Denver
Auraria Campus
Speer Boulevard and Colfax Ave.
Denver, CO 80217
www.mscd.edu/golda/

BIBLIOGRAPHY

Burkett, Elinor. Golda. New York: Harper, 2008.

"Children Help Poor in School," Milwaukee Journal, September 2, 1909, p. 4.

Gurda, John. One People, Many Paths: A History of Jewish Milwaukee. Milwaukee: Jewish Museum Milwaukee, 2009.

Hintz, Martin. Images of America: Jewish Milwaukee. Portsmouth, NH: Arcadia Publishing, 2005.

Lamers, William. Our Roots Grow Deep, 1836-1967, 2nd Edition. Milwaukee: Milwaukee Public Schools, 1974.

Meir, Golda. My Life: The Autobiography of Golda Meir. London: Futura Publications, Limited, 1976.

Correspondence with Jay Hyland, archivist, Jewish Museum Milwaukee—September 17, 2010 and June 23, 2011.

Correspondence with Dr. Norman Provizer, director of the Golda Meir Center for Political Leadership, Metropolitan State College of Denver—June 28, 2011.

Barbara Krasner enjoys writing about history – local, American, and world history, but especially Jewish history. She publishes the popular blog, *The Whole Megillah: The Writer's Resource for Jewish-Themed Story.* She runs workshops and conferences for Jewish writers at the Highlights Foundation and in conjunction with the Association of Jewish Libraries. Barbara has a B.A. in German from Douglass College, an M.B.A. in Marketing from the Rutgers Business School and an M.F.A. in Writing for Children & Young Adults from Vermont College of Fine Arts. She is the author of many articles, short stories, poems, and books. *Goldie Takes a Stand* is her first children's book.

Kelsey Garrity-Riley was born in Germany and grew up in Germany and Belgium before moving to the United States to pursue her interest in art. She received a B.F.A. from Savannah College of Art and Design and lives in Savannah, where she shares a studio with her husband. She draws inspiration from the old objects she collects, from her travels in Europe, and from daily life in the South. She works in a mix of gouache and collage with digital finishing.

Author Acknowledgments

Thank you to the Highlights Foundation for keeping a copy of Golda Meir's autobiography in the farmhouse where I read it at an Alumni Retreat. Thank you to fellow writer Lisa Idzikowski for helping me with research in Milwaukee and Jay Hyman of Milwaukee's Jewish Museum for locating the Milwaukee Journal article. Dr. Norman Provizer, Director of the Golda Meir Center for Political Leadership at Metropolitan State College of Denver, helped me ensure historical accuracy. Candace Fleming and Carolyn Yoder guided me in shaping Golda's story.